Davy Crockett
A Life on the Frontier

written by
Stephen Krensky

illustrated by
**Bob Dacey and
Debra Bandelin**

Aladdin
New York   London   Toronto   Sydney

For my nephew David —S. K.

To a delightful October visit from those irascible townsfolk
Fred and Meta, with love —B. D. & D. B.

First Aladdin edition November 2004

ALADDIN PAPERBACKS
An imprint of Simon & Schuster Children's Publishing Division
1230 Avenue of the Americas, New York, NY 10020

Book design by Lisa Vega
The text of this book was set in CenturyOldst BT.

Printed in the United States of America
2 4 6 8 10 9 7 5 3 1

The Library of Congress has cataloged the library edition as follows:
Krensky, Stephen.
Davy Crockett : a life on the frontier / written by Stephen Krensky ;
illustrated by Bob Dacey and Debra Bandelin. — 1st Aladdin Paperbacks ed.
p. cm. — (Ready-to-read)
ISBN 0-689-85945-7 (hc library ed.) — ISBN 0-689-85944-9 (pbk.)
1. Crockett, Davy, 1786–1836—Juvenile literature. 2. United States. Congress. House—
Biography—Juvenile literature. 3. Pioneers—Tennessee—Biography—Juvenile literature.
4. Legislators—United States—Biography—Juvenile literature. 5. Tennessee—Biography—
Juvenile literature. I. Dacey, Bob. II. Bandelin, Debra. III. Title. IV. Series.
F436.C95K74 2004
976.8'04'092—dc22
2004007855

Davy Crockett
A Life on the Frontier

CHAPTER ONE

The day Davy Crockett was born, the sun was so pleased, it shot straight up into the sky without a pause for morning. There was a lot to be excited about, after all. Young Davy weighed in at more than two hundred pounds. And before the day was out, he had leaped out of his crib and danced around the room.

At least that's what people said later, after Davy Crockett got famous. But Davy himself explained his birth more simply. He had actually been born "on the 17th of August, in the year 1786; whether by day or night, I believe I never heard, but if I did I have forgotten."

Davy grew up with eight brothers and sisters in the backwoods of Tennessee. Like all country boys, he learned early to hunt and fish.

When he was twelve, Davy went on a cattle drive to earn money for his family. He traveled three hundred miles before the job was done.

But then a problem developed. The drover, the man in charge, wanted Davy to keep working for him. Davy was a long way from home with little food or money. He wasn't sure what to do.

Luckily he soon met some travelers from Tennessee. The next night Davy slipped away. He walked seven miles through a snowstorm to meet up with the travelers. Once he found them, he was able to get safely started for home.

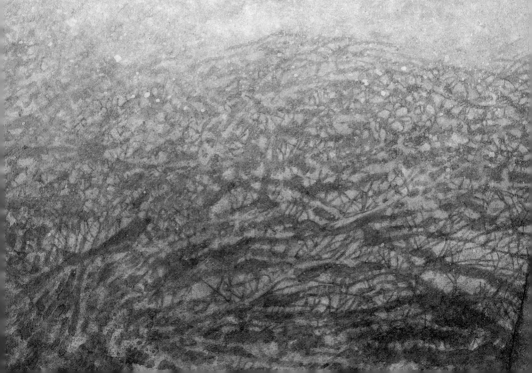

9

His family was happy to see him, and Davy was glad to see them too— at least at first. Then his father decided it was time for Davy to get some schooling. Davy wasn't very interested. In less than a week he got into a fight with an older boy.

Davy dodged going to school for the next few days. When his father found out, Davy figured he was in for a whipping. So he ran off—and didn't come back. "I knew my father's nature so well," he wrote later, "that I was certain his anger would hang on to him like a turtle does to a fisherman's toe."

Davy helped drive some cattle again and took other jobs here and there. Two years passed before he felt comfortable enough to return home.

Davy was fifteen now and almost six feet tall. He spent six months working for a farmer. The farmer's son taught school nearby and dropped in every week. Davy realized now how important it was to be able to read and write.

Davy borrowed the farmer's rifle—and discovered he was a good shot. Before long he began to win local shooting contests. But Davy wasn't satisfied, not yet. It was time for him to start aiming for other things as well.

CHAPTER TWO

One day Davy saw a raccoon up a tree. He lifted his rifle to take aim, and the raccoon didn't move. It just sat there, watching. "Why aren't you trying to run away?" Davy asked. The raccoon sighed. "Because you're Davy Crockett."

He skittered down the tree. "You never miss. I'm as good as dead already, so could you please be quick about it?"

Davy patted the raccoon on the head. "You're mighty polite," he said. "It seems a shame to waste such good manners. You should go home and bring up a whole family of respectful raccoons." The raccoon's eyes opened wide. "Why, thank you, Mister Crockett," he said—and then ran off before Davy changed his mind.

Davy didn't actually talk to the animals. Still, he knew their ways well enough. He did a lot of hunting, especially for bears. It was dangerous work. A hunter who made a mistake with a bear might never live to tell about it. But Davy was careful. Once he killed fifteen bears in just two weeks. Another time he killed more than a hundred in six months.

As much as Davy liked stretching his legs, he also wanted to settle down. He married Polly Finley in 1806, just after his twentieth birthday. The Crocketts lived in a small cabin on a farm. In the next few years they had two sons, John Wesley and William.

Meanwhile the frontier was pushing ever westward. Some of the land was uninhabited, but some was not. The Creek Indians had roamed much of the southeast for centuries. Now the pioneers were moving in on them. Even land the Creeks had been given under treaty was threatened.

So the Creeks began fighting back. Roving bands fought the settlers in scattered battles. The settlers hurried to defend themselves. Volunteers also stepped forward to serve with the army, and Davy Crockett was one of them. In 1813 and 1814 he joined campaigns that took him all the way to Florida.

The fighting was hard and uncomfortable. Davy and his men were often cold, wet, and hungry. And if his men were brave at times, so were the Indians. "The enemy met death without shrinking or complaining," he observed. "Not one asked to be spared, but fought as long as they could stand or sit."

Peace came at the end of 1814. Davy had risen to command a battalion, but he was happy to go home. "This closed my career as a warrior," he noted. "And I am glad all over that I lived to see these times, which I should not have if I had kept fooling along in war, and got used up in it."

CHAPTER THREE

One special thing about Davy was his grin. It stretched so wide it seemed to connect his ears together. He had inherited the grin from his father, John. It was said that John Crockett could grin in the teeth of a blizzard and change it into a rainbow.

Davy may have never matched that feat, but his friendly manner was very popular. After he returned home from the Indian wars, Davy was elected justice of the peace in 1817. Then he became a colonel in the county militia and also served as a town commissioner.

But life on the frontier was never predictable. Polly Crockett had gotten sick and died. Soon Davy married again. His second wife was Elizabeth Patton, a widow with two children, and they had four more children together.

In 1821 Davy ran for state legislature. Both he and his opponent gave many speeches asking for votes. After a while all the speeches started to sound alike. Davy, in fact, memorized his opponent's speech and once delivered it word for word.

The voters liked Davy's sense of humor. He was able to put their thoughts into words without a lot of fancy trappings. Davy Crockett might not have had much education, but he could represent them just fine.

After he won, Davy packed his bags for Nashville, the state capital. Everyone there wondered if he would arrive barefoot. They need not have worried.

At one dinner the governor was standing with his twelve-year-old daughter when Davy was introduced to them. "When I like a man," said Davy, "I always love his children." Then he knelt down, kissed the governor's daughter, and added, "God bless you, my child."

In 1823 Davy moved his family farther west and was again elected to the Tennessee legislature. Two years later he tried for a seat in the United States Congress. He was defeated on his first try, but he ran again in 1827.

One time during this campaign, Davy
was supposed to buy drinks for the
crowd. He went out into the woods,
shot a raccoon, and traded the coonskin
for one round of drinks. Pretty soon,
though, the crowd was thirsty again.
Davy was about to head back to
the woods when he saw his coonskin
sticking out between the logs of
the bar. He pulled it out, slapped it
on the counter, and used it to pay
for more drinks.

Newly elected Congressman David Crockett went to Washington in 1828. Newspapers reported that Davy claimed to be "half horse, half alligator, with a little touch of snapping turtle!" Supposedly he could also "outsleep, outfight, outshoot, outrun, outjump, and eat any man opposed to Jackson."

Andrew Jackson had once been Davy's commanding general. Now he was the president of the United States. They were both Tennessee men, and their lives had overlapped at times. Jackson, however, was supported by wealthy businessmen who wanted to use the wilderness to make themselves even richer.

Davy was all for a man making his fortune. Still, why should land speculators make money while hardworking farmers barely scraped by? And forcing the Indians off their land wasn't right either.

More and more, he found himself disagreeing with the president. And the president was very popular. After three terms Davy was defeated for reelection.

"I would rather be beaten and be a man," Davy declared afterward, "than to be elected and be a little puppy dog. . . . I have acted fearless and independent and I never will regret my course."

CHAPTER FOUR

One day Davy heard that a big comet was headed right for earth. "If it hits us," he was told, "we're done for." Well, Davy couldn't sit by with the world in danger. So he climbed to the top of the tallest mountain to see what he could do.

The comet came closer, all hot and fiery. Davy fired his rifle at it, but his bullets just melted in the heat.

As the comet whooshed by, all set to smash into the ground below, Davy reached out and grabbed its tail. Then he twirled the comet around and around until it got dizzy. When Davy finally let it go, the comet went flying back into the sky, fading like a spark from a dying flame.

Even though Davy Crockett didn't ever set out to save the world, he did help others and fight for what he believed in. After losing his reelection to Congress, Davy decided to try his luck in the vast open spaces of Texas. "I am in hopes," he declared, "of making a fortune yet for myself and my family."

That wasn't going to be easy. In
1835 Texas was part of Mexico. But
the Americans settling there wanted
to be free of Mexican rule, and they
were prepared to fight for their
independence. "I promised to give the
Texians a helping hand," Davy wrote,
". . . for if there is anything in this
world particularly worth living for, it
is freedom."

In early 1836 Davy found himself in San Antonio defending a former mission called the Alamo. The almost two hundred men there had been ordered to retreat because the Mexican general Santa Anna was advancing on them with almost two thousand troops. But the Alamo's defenders refused to move.

For almost two weeks they held off the Mexican advance. But on March 6, 1836, the Alamo was finally overrun. More than five hundred Mexican soldiers were killed or wounded in the attack, but all of the Alamo's defenders died as well.

And so Davy Crockett finally met his end. His tombstone, erected by his family, reads DAVY CROCKETT, PIONEER, PATRIOT, SOLDIER, TRAPPER, EXPLORER, STATE LEGISLATOR, CONGRESSMAN, MARTYRED AT THE ALAMO. 1786–1836.

He was famous for saying, "Be sure you're right, then go ahead." Davy followed his own advice, becoming a legend in his own time—and remaining one ever since.

The timeline below identifies important events in the life of Davy Crockett.

1786   Born on August 17

1798   Helps drive cattle to market for three months away from home

1799   Leaves home for two years

1806   Marries Polly Finley

1813   Volunteers to fight in Creek Indian War

1815   Marries Elizabeth Patton (after death of first wife)

1817   Takes first public office as local justice of the peace

1821   First elected to the Tennessee state legislature

1827   First elected to the United States Congress

1830   Opposes President Jackson's Indian Resettlement Act

1834   Publishes his autobiography

1835   Defeated in congressional election, leaves for Texas

1836   Dies at the Alamo on March 6